All About
Roberto Clemente

Andrew Conte

BLUE RIVER PRESS
Indianapolis, Indiana

All About Roberto Clemente
Copyright © 2016 Andrew Conte

Published by Blue River Press
Indianapolis, Indiana
www.brpressbooks.com

Distributed by Cardinal Publishers Group
Tom Doherty Company, Inc.
www.cardinalpub.com

ISBN: 978-1-68157-089-1

Author: Andrew Conte
Series Editor: Charleen Davis
Editor: Dani McCormick
Interior Illustrator: Bryan Janky
Book Design: Dave Reed
Cover Artist: Jennifer Mujezinovic
Cover Design: David Miles

Printed in the United States of America

Contents

Preface   vii

1. Growing Up in Sugar   1

2. Turning Pro   14

3. Becoming a Pirate   24

4. Giving Back   35

5. Answering Questions   42

6. Being the Most Valuable   57

7. Leaving It All   72

8. Getting on Board   81

9. Living On   95

Select Quotes from Roberto Clemente   103

Roberto Clemente Timeline   104

World Timeline   105

Glossary   108

Bibliography   111

Index   112

For John David

Roberto Clemente loved baseball
but didn't know his passion and courage
would change the game forever

All About
Roberto Clemente

Preface

Roberto Clemente often dreamed that he would die in a plane crash. The nightmares frightened him, but he could not let them stop him. He had too many things he wanted to do. He worried he would not have enough time.

Born on the Caribbean island of Puerto Rico in 1934, Roberto often felt like he had two strikes against him.

His skin was very dark at a time when many Americans treated people differently based on the color of their skin. Growing up, he thought of himself only as Puerto Rican. But when he arrived in the United States, people told him he was black. People who did not know anything about him were mean to him just because his skin looked dark to them. For the first time, Roberto started to see himself differently.

Like many people in Puerto Rico, Roberto grew up speaking Spanish. When he came to the United

States, most Americans spoke only English. He could not communicate his feelings or even ask for directions or help. Worse, when he tried to speak English, many Americans made fun of the way he talked because they could not understand his thick accent. They laughed at how he misused words. Roberto felt isolated and lonely.

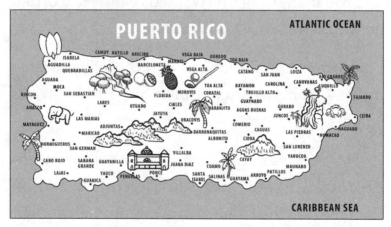

Puerto Rico, though small, was full of activity, talent, and beauty

When people misunderstood Roberto, he resolved to start speaking with his body. He could play baseball. Many said he played the game better than anyone they ever had seen. So while people made fun of Roberto for the color of his skin or the way he talked, he worked at playing the game the best that he could. He hit the ball farther. He ran the bases faster. When the ball came to him in right field, he would pick it up and throw it back harder than almost anyone. No one laughed at the way Roberto played baseball. Instead, they cheered for him and called out his name. Many of those who first had laughed at Roberto realized they had been wrong.

It was not enough to just play the game well. Roberto had been very poor as a child. Even as he started making money from baseball, Roberto remembered what it had been like on the island when he had to make his own baseball equipment from whatever he could find. He knew that many children back home still could not afford gloves, bats, and baseballs. He remembered that for some, it would be hard just to find enough to eat or a safe place to sleep at night.

As he started becoming a famous athlete, Roberto wanted to help others. He handed out money to people who needed it. He visited sick children in the hospital. He bought food and clothing for people who could not afford them.

When he traveled home to his island of Puerto Rico, he worked hard to show the Puerto Ricans that he also had not forgotten them. He showed the people who laughed at him that they should treat others the way they wanted to be treated.

"I want to be remembered as a ballplayer who gave all he had to give," Roberto once said.

Maybe he really did know that he would not have much time.

Roberto was the Pirates star player,
but he had to fight hard to get there

Chapter 1
<u>Growing Up in Sugar</u>

Roberto Clemente Walker was born on August 18, 1934, on the island of Puerto Rico. It takes a couple of hours to fly there from Florida, but the island is a part of the United States called a territory. Roberto was both American and Puerto Rican.

Puerto Rico is a US territory and one of the Carribean islands just southeast of Florida

He also had the last names of his father and mother—Clemente and Walker—although most people in the United States knew him only by his father's name.

Roberto's father, Melchor, carried a radio and a boxed lunch with him on his way to work in the fields where he earned less than $2 per day

Roberto's father, Melchor Clemente, worked as a foreman in the sugar fields behind their house. Before the sun came up most mornings, Melchor woke up and started walking to work. He wore a straw hat and carried a transistor radio. Melchor was in charge of other workers and he made twice as much money, but he earned only about twelve dollars a week.

Roberto's mother, Luisa Walker, worked at home. She sewed and made lunches for the workers in the sugar fields. She ran a small market out of the family's house, selling milk, flour, rice and eggs. Sometimes when she sold meat, Luisa would buy a beef carcass, throw it into a wheelbarrow and take it home to butcher into smaller pieces that could be sold. She had a very strong right arm.

Roberto was the baby of his family, five years younger than any of his siblings. He had two half-siblings, a brother and a sister, from his mother's first marriage before her husband died. Roberto's half-brother, Luis Oquendo, was 18 years old when Roberto was born. When

Luisa married Melchor, they first had three sons—
Osvaldo, Justino and Andres. Justino was six years
older than Roberto and taught him how to play

Roberto's mother, Luisa, made and sold food
to help make money for the large family

baseball. Roberto always told people later in life that his brother had been a better player but did not get the chance to play in the major leagues.

Roberto also had a sister, Anairis. When Roberto was just an infant, she died in a gasoline explosion near an outdoor stove. She was only five years old. Roberto did not remember her, but he often said that he felt her presence throughout his life.

Whenever someone asked him a question or wanted him to do some chore, Roberto would answer by saying, *"Momentito,"* or give me a moment. He said it so often that the children started calling him "Momen" and the name stuck.

The family lived in a wooden house with five rooms. With so many children, some slept in every room. Roberto grew up at a time called the Great Depression when a lot of adults could not find jobs and many children did not have enough to eat. His family was lucky because his father had a job. His mother made extra money, and they always had enough food. They were not rich, but they were not poor. Their house had electricity and a little box above the kitchen that caught rain water for drinking and washing.

Roberto's family lived in a small house with electricity, a luxury during the Great Depression

Children on the island played baseball—even when they did not have a bat, a baseball, gloves or a field. They made those items out of whatever they could find. Roberto often swung a tree branch or a broom handle as a bat. His friends tossed an old can as the ball or tied old rags together to make one. Rough cloth bags used for holding coffee beans could be turned into mitts with a little cushioning inside. And the street in

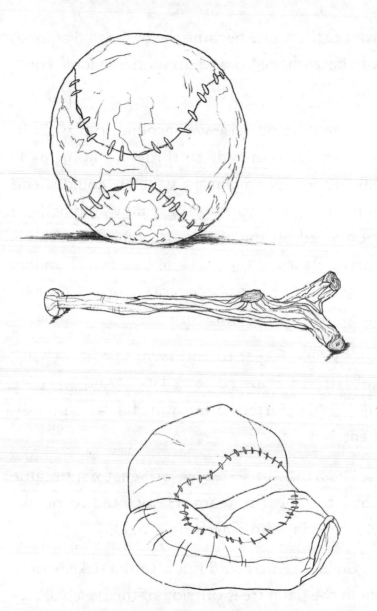

Roberto often played baseball with improvised
equipment, like rag balls,
stick bats, and burlap sack gloves

front of the house became the baseball diamond, with bases made from whatever the children could find.

Even if no one else was around to play, Roberto would go outside to throw his homemade ball in the air or against a wall. He could spend hours that way, tossing the ball, watching how it bounced off the wall and catching it with his hands. He loved the game of baseball so much. Sometimes Roberto's parents worried that he loved the game too much.

"I would forget to eat because of baseball," Roberto remembered years later. "And one time my mother started to burn my bat as a punishment."

The San Juan *Senadores*, or Senators, became Roberto's favorite team. He wanted to be like Monte Irvin, who played right field.

Children who could not afford a ticket would climb the palm trees outside of the baseball stadium, sitting high among the fronds, so they could see the action. Roberto often had enough money to get inside. Children could earn pennies by carrying water into the sugarcane fields for the workers, and Roberto would work hard to make the money so he could attend the games. Often his father would give him the money too—ten cents for the bus, and fifteen cents for a ticket.

Roberto and his friends often carried water to the field workers to earn money to buy baseball tickets

Roberto always sat near the outfield so he could watch Irvin. Even though Roberto was too shy to look at Irvin in the face, the player noticed him always sitting there. Irvin started talking with

Roberto. If they saw each other before the game, Irvin would give the young boy his uniform bag to carry so he could get into the stadium for free.

Roberto always sat near the outfield so he could watch his hero, Monte Irvin, play right field

Roberto studied everything about the player— the way he walked and ran, how he stood on the grass and how his arm moved during his strong throw from the outfield. Roberto watched how Irvin would wait for the ball to bounce off the outfield wall, catch it in his glove, quickly turn and rocket the ball toward the infield with his arm. Irvin seemed to make complicated plays look simple, with one graceful motion. Roberto noticed, too, that Irvin took the time to be nice to his fans.

When he turned fourteen, Roberto started playing softball for a team called Sello Rojo, which means red stamp or seal. The team was named for a company that sold rice and had a red stamp on its bags. A man who worked for the company saw Roberto playing and recruited him. Two years later, Roberto started playing baseball for an amateur team.

Melchor, Roberto's father, had never played baseball and he had never even seen anyone play the game. When he watched his son playing for the first time, he became angry. He did not understand what the players were doing. Other boys hit the ball, ran toward first base and then went back to the bench to sit down. When Roberto hit the ball, he usually had to keep running around the bases.

Roberto's parents did not believe that he could play baseball for his career. His mother wanted him to stay in school and study civil engineering, learning how to build roads, bridges and buildings. His father thought baseball was a distraction. When Roberto had a chance to be paid for playing baseball, his parents were worried because he had not finished school. But the team said Roberto could go to school while playing.

As Luisa and Melchor saw their son becoming successful, they realized that Roberto worked

Roberto played softball with Sello Rojo,
a Puerto Rican amateur team

hard at playing baseball. It was a job, and he was good at it. They were very proud of him for following his passion.

Chapter 2
<u>Turning Pro</u>

By the time he turned eighteen, Roberto became so good at baseball that a local professional team wanted him to play. The team was called *Cangrejeros de Santurce*, or the Santurce Crabbers. The manager was known as the "Big Crab."

The manager of a local team, "Big Crab," saw Roberto playing and recruited him to the professional Puerto Rican team the *Cangrejeros de Santurce*

The team paid Roberto a seven hundred dollar signing bonus and forty dollars a week. The Crabbers' games were broadcast across the island by a radio station so Roberto had a chance to start becoming famous. People who listened to the games started to recognize Roberto's name. The team won the island championship in Roberto's first year, but he did not play much. He often sat on the bench and only went into games when the team needed him.

While Roberto was still in high school, scouts from the Dodgers Major League Baseball team came to the island to look for players. Teams from the United States seemed so far away that Roberto did not even dream about playing for them. But he went anyway with about seventy other boys to try out.

The scouts liked what they saw. Word got out and other teams started looking for Roberto too. Soon, five Major League Baseball teams wanted him. The Milwaukee Braves offered him the most money—$25,000—but Roberto wanted to play in New York where he had family and friends.

The Dodgers were based in Brooklyn, New York. They offered Roberto a $10,000 bonus and $5,000 a year. Melchor, Roberto's father, sent the team a telegram: "I will sign a contract on behalf of my son..."

The company that made Louisville Slugger bats asked Roberto if he needed any equipment. They sent him a bat with the signature "Momen Clemente."

But the Dodgers did not bring Roberto to New York. The manager wanted him to start out playing in the minor leagues first. The team assigned him to play for the Royals, the Dodgers' minor league affiliate in the Canadian city of Montreal, Quebec.

Roberto quickly became homesick. For the first time, he was a long distance away from the wooden house where he grew up. The weather felt different, cooler with gray skies. The food tasted different. He could not find his favorite dishes: rice, beans and plantains.

Scouts from professional US teams were impressed
when they came to watch Roberto play

Most people in Montreal speak French, but
Roberto could not. People on his island spoke
Spanish, and he had studied only a little English in
school. He could not even tell anyone how he felt.

The Dodgers were not ready for Roberto to
play in New York. But they did not want any other
teams to see him playing in Montreal. If he stayed
in the minors, any other club could draft him. The

Dodgers tried to hide Roberto by not letting him start in many games or take a lot of turns batting.

If another team sent a scout to watch the Royals, the manager would not let Roberto play. He would have to sit on the bench and watch the other players. One time the manager even pulled Roberto out of the game in the first inning with the bases loaded. If Roberto played too well, other teams might try to draft him away from the Dodgers.

Roberto became frustrated. He felt ready to quit baseball. He just wanted to go home to his island. As he was getting ready to leave, someone from the baseball team saw him. They explained why the Dodgers wanted to keep him a secret. Roberto was still mad, but he agreed to stay until the season ended.

That winter, Roberto finally went home to Puerto Rico. He played again for the Crabbers. That year, the Dodgers' owners pulled together some of the best players in baseball. They signed Willie Mays, the New York Giants' famous center fielder.

After having such a bad time in Montreal, Roberto was thrilled to be back playing in front of his fans. The team put so much fear into opponents that people started calling them *"el Escuadrón del Pánico,"* or the Squadron of Panic. The Crabbers won the island championship and the Caribbean World Series. Many believe it was the best Caribbean team ever.

When he signed a contract to play with the Dodgers minor league team, Roberto had been in high school. He had not finished his classes. Now he went back to school eager to earn his graduation and have his diploma.

While Roberto was still on the island, the owners and managers of all the major league teams met to draft players. The Pittsburgh Pirates had the worst record the previous season, so they had the first pick.

Even though the Dodgers had tried to hide Roberto, they could not keep him a secret. A scout for the Pirates had seen him playing in Montreal. The scout excitedly told the team in Pittsburgh they should take Roberto in the draft.

The Pirates' general manager was a man named Branch Rickey. A few years earlier, Rickey had been with the Dodgers when he decided to put an African American named Jackie Robinson on his team. Until that point, Major League Baseball had only white players. African Americans had to play on their own teams in the Negro Leagues. Some of the teams were very good and the players believed they could play against the best athletes in the world. But until 1947, when Robinson started for the Dodgers at second base, players with dark skin never got the chance.

Now Rickey was running the team in Pittsburgh. He had a chance to help make history again. The major leagues still had only a few African Americans. It had even fewer players from Latin America who spoke Spanish.

The Pirates had fielded a Puerto Rican player named Carlos Bernier two years earlier and the team had added an African American, Curt Roberts, that season. Roberto had dark skin and he spoke Spanish. Rickey knew he could help break down another barrier by choosing him. Once fans saw how well Roberto could play, they would start to feel less prejudice against players who looked or talked differently. They would realize the most important thing was how that person could play the game.

Jackie Robinson broke the barrier between African Americans and professional baseball in 1947

But that was not the main reason the Pirates wanted Roberto. The team desperately needed good players. The scouts had seen Roberto play in Montreal. They knew he could play the game.

Branch Rickey chose Roberto because he was a great baseball player, but he also wanted to break another barrier in baseball

People in the draft room gasped when Pirates General Manager Branch Rickey called out Roberto Clemente's name. Many of the newspaper reporters did not know anything about the player. They worried that the Pirates had made another mistake. But scouts for other teams realized the

Pirates had chosen wisely. The other scouts had seen Roberto play too and his name topped many of their wish lists. They knew the Pirates had just stolen the best player.

Roberto was still in Puerto Rico when he found out the Pirates picked him. He was glad to be going to a team that wanted him. But he had one problem, he didn't know where Pittsburgh was!

Chapter 3
<u>Becoming a Pirate</u>

Factories in Pittsburg made steel, shooting out fiery orange flames and dark, thick smoke.

Metal is needed to make cars and airplanes, refrigerators and washing machines. The mills in Pittsburgh and Western Pennsylvania made steel beams for the Empire State Building in New York, the Arch in St. Louis and the Bay Bridge in San Francisco.

But the factories made a mess too. The air was so dirty that the smoke blocked out the sun and street lights stayed on during the day. Men who wore white shirts to work in Pittsburgh's downtown offices had to change them at lunch because they turned gray with soot. Pittsburgh would be very different from Puerto Rico.

Before Roberto could get to the city, he ran into some bad luck. The Pirates had paid him a $4,000 bonus and he bought a new blue car. After a game with the Crabbers, Roberto was driving along a dark mountain road late at night. The driver of another car went through a red light and hit Roberto's car. When an ambulance came, Roberto said he felt fine even though his neck and back hurt him a little. That pain would linger for years.

Pittsburgh was primarily an industrial factory town, which was very different from the un-industrial island of Puerto Rico

The Pirates practiced in Florida for several weeks before the season, and Roberto went there to meet his new teammates. For the first time, he realized people were going to treat him differently because of his skin color.

At home, Roberto considered himself Puerto Rican. He had dark skin, but that did not matter. When he arrived in Florida, people said Roberto was black like an African American. He did not know what that meant, but he quickly found that it limited where he could go and what he could do.

Most of Roberto's teammates were white. They stayed at a fancy hotel near the beach. They ate in nice restaurants and spent their free time swimming or playing golf at a country club. People with dark skin, like Roberto, could not stay in the same hotel. Florida had strict rules that limited where people with dark skin could go or what they could do. He had to find a local family that would let him sleep in an extra room.

He could not eat in the same restaurants either. When the team stopped to eat after a game, Roberto had to wait on the bus and white players would bring him food. Blacks could not swim with whites. Roberto could not even enter the golf course or the country club.

Whenever he went out in public in Southern states, Roberto could not use the same bathrooms or drink from the same water fountains. They had signs saying which ones he could use. People with dark skin could not use the ones marked "whites." They could use only the ones marked "coloreds."

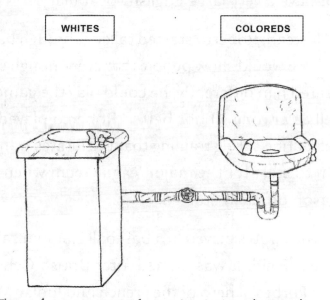

These famous water fountains in North Carolina represented the segregation that Roberto and his other non-white teammates had to endure

Roberto never before thought of himself as different. Now it made him feel angry and embarrassed that he could not do the same things as his white teammates. The whole system seemed unfair.

But once again, Roberto could not tell people how he felt. He did not know the words. Very few people in Florida spoke Spanish, and Roberto did not have a very large English vocabulary.

Instead, Roberto started talking through baseball. He would show people that even though they treated him differently, he could play the game as well as anyone—if not better. Roberto played so well during spring training that the Pirates wanted him to start for the major league team when the season officially started.

The Pirates played in a baseball stadium called Forbes Field. It was named after British General John Forbes, a hero of the French and Indian War. His troops fought for the land around Pittsburgh and Forbes named the city after capturing it from the French.

The Forbes Field was named after General John Forbes, a hero of the French and Indian War

Ballplayers dressed in a locker room beneath the stadium. The building was old and had opened in 1909. The locker room was dark and damp. Roberto was frightened of the rats that ran around down there.

But when he headed toward the field, Roberto could smell the freshly cut green grass. The stadium had been built into the city blocks. Roberto could see the University of Pittsburgh's

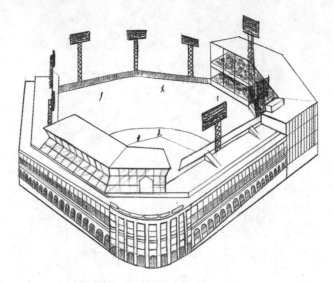

Forbes Field sat in the middle of Pittsburgh, though it was demolished in 1971, the outfield wall still stands

Cathedral of Learning skyscraper looming over the outfield wall. Everything had been so strange since he left Puerto Rico, but right field felt like home!

Roberto started out hot. He was playing well and getting used to his new team. But then his luck ran out. He kept hitting the ball hard, but he was hitting the ball right toward the players in the field. The other teams kept getting him out. Roberto grew so frustrated that one time he threw his batting helmet on the ground and it broke in half.

Like many players, Roberto felt superstitious. He believed that little things could affect the way he played. If he had a good game, he would keep wearing the same shirt for days. Once when a teammate touched him before a game, he had played well—and then insisted that the other player always touch him before games.

Now, Roberto wanted to figure out what was wrong. Someone suggested that his number was unlucky. Roberto had been wearing number 13.

Immediately, he called out to the team trainer for a new shirt. Later people would say that Roberto added up all of the letters in his name—Roberto Clemente Walker and asked for number 21. But in reality, that was the only shirt left. Roberto's number would become famous.

When he wasn't playing baseball, Roberto had lots of free time. He would practice speaking English by going to the movies and repeating the actors' lines: "You go into town. I'll meet you at the canyon."

A family living near the ballpark rented a room to Roberto. He was eating all of his meals at restaurants, but he could smell the food from the kitchen in the house. He missed his mother's cooking.

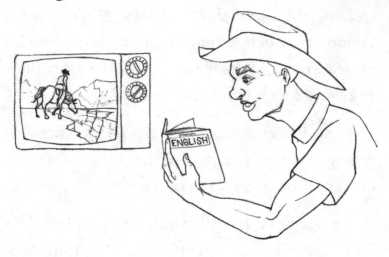

Roberto practiced and improved his English by watching movies and repeating after the actors

Roberto longed for some of the simple dishes from the island. Red beans cooked in a thick sauce and served over rice; *morcilla,* a sausage made with blood, rice and spices; *mofongo,* a dish made with smashed plantains around crab, shrimp or other meat; and breadfruit and yuca, starchy vegetables similar to potatoes, were not available in Pittsburgh.

One day, Roberto came home with an armful of steaks, beans, fruits, vegetables and rice. He asked the woman who owned the house if she would cook them. She did and Roberto ate that night with the family. He started feeling that the woman and man were like adopted parents. They saw him as their son.

The Pirates players took the team name to heart. Many of them acted like real pirates, with rough, loud voices. They were always looking for a good time. Roberto was not like the others. He was quiet and shy. But he started playing better and his teammates started counting on him. They knew he could throw the ball from right field harder than almost anyone. And while he did not often hit home runs, Roberto had developed a habit of getting the ball into play.

Still, the fans in Pittsburgh did not understand Roberto. They saw his dark skin and made fun of the way he talked when he tried speaking English. When he batted, people would call out mean things from the stands: "Hit him in the head!" It seemed so strange.

One day when a reporter asked Roberto about the people who yelled at him, he finally said what he had been thinking.

"I don't believe in color," Roberto said. "I believe in people. I always respect everyone, and thanks to God, my mother and my father taught me never to hate, never to dislike someone because of their color. I didn't even know about this stuff when I got here."

He decided then to show people they were wrong. He would become the best player he could—and he would treat everyone with respect.

Chapter 4
Giving Back

With the money he made from baseball, Roberto bought his parents a house in Puerto Rico. Unlike the place where he had grown up, it would have lots of rooms and modern comforts— electricity, running water and air conditioning.

When Roberto returned to the island, though, he would go back to his old neighborhood to go visit his old friends. He wanted people to know that he had not changed, even if he was playing baseball in the United States and making money. Roberto never forgot who he was or where he came from.

The poor country people in Puerto Rico are known as *jíbaro*. Roberto loved them. He remembered what it had been like to grow up without a lot of things, when he had to make his own bat, glove and ball out of whatever he could find.

When he was a child, the dream of playing in the United States seemed too much to even think about. But Roberto wanted to show the people of the island—especially the children—that they could become whatever they wanted. If they dreamed big and worked hard for it, they could be like him.

Roberto gave back to the people of Puerto Rico. Often he would hand out coins to poor people on the street and stop to ask them about their lives. If he saw children playing baseball, he would stop and give them free lessons on how to get better. If someone told him their back hurt, he might talk with them about his own pain and how he tried to make it go away.

As his English started getting better, Roberto used his words to let people in the United States know it wasn't fair to treat others differently because of the color of their skin or where they had been born. "Everyone knows I've been struggling all my life," Roberto said in one of his speeches. "I believe that every human being is equal, but one has to fight hard all the time to maintain that equality."

Jackie Robinson had been the first African American to play in Major League Baseball. Now many Latino athletes started to see Roberto as their leader, someone like Robinson. They saw him making sacrifices to work harder and to not let people's meanness affect him. They knew he remained faithful to his island.

When he saw other Latinos, Roberto would tell them to hold their heads up and to be proud of their language and customs. He had been among the first Latinos to play baseball in the United States, but he believed that someday many Latinos would play the game. And many of them would enter baseball's hall of fame.

Roberto loved children and would donate food, clothes, money, and sports equipment when he visited Puerto Rico

Roberto's baseball locker was neat, but he always had
a little honey to share with the other player's children

For young Spanish-speaking men and women throughout the Caribbean, Roberto was a pioneer. He was creating a path for Latinos to follow.

Roberto especially liked children. Adults had treated him badly, but children seemed to understand him.

Before games, Roberto had started a ritual of eating a spoonful of honey—for health and for good luck. If the son or daughter of another player or team worker came into the dressing room, Roberto would reach into his locker and pull out the honey. Soon he would be sharing it.

Sick children in other cities would look at the baseball schedule to see when the Pirates were coming to town. They would send Roberto letters asking him to visit them in the hospital. Often he would—bringing them a signed baseball or just stopping to talk. Roberto always tried to make time for his fans.

When he had free time in Pittsburgh, Roberto often would visit the local YMCA to talk with young athletes and mentor them on how to play sports and stay in shape. He never forgot what it had been like growing up and dreaming of playing in front of a stadium filled with fans.

Roberto loved when his young fans sent him letters asking him to come visit them and often visited sick children in hospitals

Roberto had a big dream of building a place in Puerto Rico where young people could learn and practice. Roberto wanted to create a "sports city" for the children of his island where they could play baseball and other sports. In his mind, the place would have lots of fields, a swimming pool, a gymnasium and weight rooms. It would have all of the things he did not have as a child.

Roberto knew it was a big dream. He did not know if he could ever make it happen.

Chapter 5
<u>Answering Questions</u>

Even after making it to the major league with the Pirates, Roberto remained an enigma to many fans. They did not know just how good he might be. Many of the white reporters continued to ignore him, and Roberto had not played as well as he could. At the end of his first season, one newspaper said his hitting remained a "question mark."

Roberto's first season was not his best
and his hitting was labeled a "question mark"
by one reporter in 1956

Soon, Roberto started making people notice. In his second season, his batting average improved and he made plays no one ever had seen before. "Several times this season, he has come up with catches nobody on the bench figured he'd ever make," his manager told the press. "He's also taught runners in the league not to take any chances with his arm. He throws like a rifle."

Roberto noticed something about the fans too. When he made an incredible play in the outfield or came up with a big hit, teammates and fans forgot he couldn't speak English well or that his skin was dark. He was just a baseball player. That made Roberto smile.

Things were not always easy though. Roberto felt pain in his back and neck from the car accident in Puerto Rico years earlier. Doctors looked at him and could not see anything wrong. But Roberto could feel it. Many people did not believe Roberto when he said his body hurt.

Sometimes the pain made it hard for him to swing at the ball and he sometimes needed to miss a game. That made many fans disappointed and angry. In his third season, Roberto nearly quit baseball again. He had his tonsils removed, lost fifteen pounds, spent time in the hospital and missed a month of games.

Though he tried not to show it, Roberto had a painful back injury that sometimes interfered with his playing

Teammates questioned Roberto's toughness. Some started saying he was "jaking it"—clubhouse slang for pretending to be injured so he would not have to work so hard. When Roberto heard what they were saying, it made him mad. He thought about going back to Puerto Rico. There, people always had understood him and trusted him.

A lot of the newspaper reporters still made fun of his accent. They wrote his quotes phonetically—how they sounded—rather than how they were spelled.

"No one knows what eet is," Roberto told a reporter one day. "They can't find anything. I run, I throw, I move, eet hurts. Some day eet hurt, some day no. If eet doesn't cure, I quit. I no fool around."

Roberto did not quit baseball. He played through the pain and eventually he started to feel better. Within a few years, he was becoming known as a reliable player—with his consistent hits and strong arm.

The Pirates had a radio announcer, Bill Prince, who liked to come up with funny ways of talking about the game. When the Pirates won a close game, he'd say, "We had 'em all the way." If a batter hit a home run, he would tell the listeners, "You can kiss it goodbye."

Bill Prince greeted Roberto at the plate
with a loud "Arriba! Arriba!"

One day he heard a Spanish teammate call-ing out to Roberto, *"Arriba! Arriba!"* That was a Spanish way of saying, Go! Go! The announcer started using it himself every time Roberto came to the plate, and fans started calling it out too.

Over Roberto's first five seasons, the Pirates had been terrible. But the players felt like they were getting better. By the spring of 1960, they believed it. The Pirates started winning games. Instead of drifting to the bottom again, they lead the league.

Roberto started having hitting streaks, getting hits in nine consecutive games one time. His fielding made people talk too. One time, Roberto ran full speed and caught the ball just as he hit the brick outfield wall. He needed six stitches in his chin but he held onto the ball. The Pirates won the game too, 1 to 0. Fans started thinking about Roberto as a baseball player and unique athlete, rather than just someone with dark skin and a funny accent.

"We have good speerit on Pirates thees year," Roberto told another reporter. "Everybody try little harder and make it harder for the other team. ... We hungry to win ball games and fly pennant flag in Forbes Field. If nobody get sick, we make it a race all the time."

Roberto's speed helped him stretch how many bases he could get off a single hit, which helped win games

In those days, Major League Baseball did not have playoffs. The one team with the best record in the National League and the one team in the American League each won a pennant. Those two teams played in the World Series. The first team that won four out of seven games would be the champion.

On the last day of the 1960 season, the Pirates were in Milwaukee when they won the pennant with the best record in the National League. When the team plane arrived back in Pittsburgh, thousands of fans were waiting at the airport. Thousands more stood along city streets as they players paraded past. The Pirates had not won the pennant in thirty-three years. The fans thought this might be as good as it could get.

That year, the New York Yankees won the American League pennant. The Yankees had won the pennant twenty times in the years when the Pirates had not won any. Most people thought the Yankees would win the World Series too.

The Pirates believed in themselves. "We'll fight 'em until our teeth fall out," the team's third baseman said, "and then we'll grab 'em with our gums."

The Yankees had a simple strategy for Roberto. Their pitcher would throw the ball at his head one time to scare him. They figured he would be too afraid to get back up and keep swinging.

Roberto did not worry about what others said or did. The fans in Pittsburgh had finally embraced him. They named him their favorite Pirates player that year. He knew at least some people were starting finally to see him truly for himself.

All of Pittsburgh seemed to have black-and-gold fever, for the team's colors. A popular song played on the radio using the team's nickname, the Bucs: "Oh, the Bucs are going all the way, all the way, all the way. Oh, the Bucs are going all the way, all the way this year. Beat 'em, Bucs!"

Fans hung signs around town, saying, "Beat 'em, Bucs!" Inside Forbes Field, red, white and blue fabric hung around the upper deck of the ballpark, reminding everyone of baseball's place as America's favorite pastime.

The Pirates won the first game, 6 to 4, but remained the underdogs in the best-of-seven series. When the Yankees won games, they won big. The Yankees took the second game by a score of 16 to 3 and the third game by 10 to 0.

Pittsburgh did not give up. The Bucs narrowly won the next two games, 3 to 2 and 5 to 2. The Yankees tied up the series by winning the sixth game, 12 to 0.

Every time the Pirates lost, they had been crushed. But each team had won three games. The Pirates and Yankees would play a seventh game in Pittsburgh to determine the World Series champion. The fans did not know which Pirates team would show up: The one that barely won games—or the one that lost big. The fans knew the Pirates would have to play at their best and keep the score close if they hoped to win.

The World Series had been especially important to Roberto. His games were being shown in Puerto Rico for the first time. He joked about wearing cologne so he would smell good for his fans watching on TV back home.

The Yankees scouts had been wrong about Roberto. He had not been afraid. He had gotten a hit in every game of the series, and his throws from right field had frightened Yankees runners.

They knew he could get them out at third base or home with a strong play.

Game seven seemed like a microcosm of the entire series. The Pirates quickly scored four runs to take the lead, but then the Yankees came back with one run in the fifth inning and four more in the sixth to take the lead. The Yankees scored two more runs in the top of the eighth inning. It looked like they would crush the Pirates again.

In the bottom of the eighth inning the Pirates came out swinging. They scored five runs. That put them ahead 9 to 7. They had to get only three outs in the top of the ninth inning to win the series.

The Yankees were not done yet either. They scored two runs in the top of the ninth to tie the game again. The Pirates needed one more run.

Bill Mazeroski, the Pirates' second baseman, had grown up near Pittsburgh. His father had worked in a coal mine, like many of the Pittsburgh fans. People in the city had needed some time to get to know Roberto. But it seemed like they always had known the player everyone called "Maz."

The Yankees were the favorite for the 1960 World Series because they played well together and were coming from a great season

As the second half of the ninth inning started, the Yankees took the field. Fans in the stands stood at their seats cheering, while people across the city listened on radios to see what would happen. Maz put on his batting helmet, picked up his bat and walked toward home plate. It was his turn to bat.

The first pitch sailed high for a ball. The second pitch came over the plate. Maz swung and connected.

The ball headed toward the left field wall, and Maz ran hard for first base. The left fielder turned to play the ball if it bounced off of the ivy-covered outfield wall.

Teammates and fans alike ran onto the field to cheer Bill Mazeroski to home plate for the World Series win

It didn't. The ball carried over the wall for a home run.

As Maz rounded second, he started waving his helmet in the air and skipping. Roberto and the other players ran out of the dugout to crowd around home plate. Fans rushed out of the stands onto the field. A couple of them ran beside Maz as he turned for home.

The underdog Pirates won the World Series with a final home run. In the locker room, the players kept celebrating. Roberto smiled broadly but he stayed quiet and quickly dressed. He had to catch a plane to New York and then back to Puerto Rico. He grabbed the box with his trophy for being the fans' favorite player and walked outside.

A fan noticed him and called out. Others quickly crowded around. They wanted to touch him and congratulate him. It took Roberto an hour to walk a few feet to a friend's car. He smiled the entire time. It had taken the fans in Pittsburgh a long time to get to know Roberto. But when they watched him play baseball, they saw how hard he worked and how much he loved the game. They came to love Roberto.

Then later that night when his plane landed in Puerto Rico, Roberto looked out and could not believe it. Thousands of people waited for him there too. The fans on the island had been watching Roberto play baseball since he was a boy. Now they held signs and called out his name. Many danced a Latino dance called the salsa.

The fans had seen him on TV and they felt pride. He was the first Latino baseball player to win a World Series. The whole island wanted to congratulate him, and people in many Spanish-speaking countries felt good about his success. Roberto smiled again. But he felt a little angry inside too.

Chapter 6
Being the Most Valuable

Even as a champion, Roberto felt disappointed. He believed he was the most valuable player. But the reporters who voted for the winner chose one his teammates instead. Roberto finished eighth in the voting. He was not even close to winning.

"I drove in more runs, and I hit more balls, and I helped win more games," Roberto told a reporter. "... The writers made me feel bad."

Thinking about the next season, Roberto wanted to play even harder. He wanted to be the most valuable on the field. Off the field, he wanted to feel valuable too.

A few years earlier, the United States had started fighting a war in Korea, and Roberto had to join the military. He became a U.S. Marine. He missed part of a season to take basic training, but was able to keep playing.

Roberto joined the marines in 1958,
missing part of a season

On a trip back to the island, Roberto met a girl. Her name was Vera Cristina Zabala, and he fell in love with her very quickly. Roberto had met many girls, but Vera seemed special because she was not only very pretty but also had a strong spirit. She reminded Roberto of home and she loved the island like he did.

Before they could start dating, Roberto had to get permission from Vera's father to talk with her. When they did start spending time together, Roberto and Vera realized they had a lot in common and talked for hours. Even when he came back to Pittsburgh to play baseball, Roberto thought about Vera and he called her often on the phone.

Before long, Roberto asked Vera to marry him, and they had a big wedding on the island.

Roberto married Puerto Rico native
Vera Cristina Zabala in 1964

Their first son, Roberto Jr., was born on August 17, 1965, the day before his father turned thirty-one. Less than a year later, they had a second son, Luis Roberto. And four years after that, in

1970, they had a third son, Enrique Roberto. Vera and the boys lived with Roberto in Pittsburgh, but each time Vera became pregnant, Roberto insisted she return to the island to give birth. He wanted his sons to be born in Puerto Rico. Like their parents, the boys would be American and Puerto Rican.

Roberto was proud to be an American, but he was proud to be from the island too. He was proud of his culture. And he was proud of his people. He never stopped thinking about Puerto Rico.

"For him, being born in the island had that flavor," his son Roberto Jr. said years later. "You're born and you're raised there. That's how he wanted it to be." Being valuable to Roberto meant inspiring Latino athletes too. He could not become good at just baseball while forgetting about his heritage.

With the Pirates, Roberto fought against racism. When major league players formed a union to ask the owners for higher pay and more rights,

Roberto became a leader of the group. He wanted black players to be treated better.

Roberto took his job as a father seriously and took his wife and sons with him everywhere

Whenever he got angry about being treated differently because of his skin color, Roberto thought about Dr. Martin Luther King. The Civil Rights leader believed in nonviolent resistance—showing people it was wrong to segregate African Americans from whites, but not fighting back physically. Roberto respected King and they became friends.

Roberto still felt angry about how he was treated when the Pirates went to Florida for spring training. Florida still had strict rules that prevented people with dark-colored skin from doing the same things as people with light-colored skin. He complained about having to wait on the bus for food while the white players ate inside restaurants. The team bought a station wagon for the black players, so they could drive on their own and eat in a place that allowed blacks. It was an improvement. But it was not equal treatment. Roberto wanted all of his teammates to be able to eat, sleep and play together, in the same places. He kept pushing.

"He became an activist," his son Roberto Jr. said. "He became a voice. That fueled him to take action and be outspoken about the issues and the problems he was seeing in society as well as in baseball."

Dr. Martin Luther King Jr. inspired Roberto to fight for equality inside and outside of baseball

All of the players—whites and blacks—finally agreed they did not want to be separated for eating, sleeping or anything. The players' union demanded that owners find a way to stop segregating the players by color. They wanted baseball teams to push Florida's towns to change their rules.

Before the next season, the Pirates purchased a dormitory in Florida. It was not as fancy as the beachfront hotel, but all of the players could finally stay together—even if a white hotel owner would not allow it. All of the teammates, white and black, could be in the same place.

At the same time that Roberto was fighting for the rights of baseball players with dark skin, Americans were struggling with issues of race too. The United States Congress passed the Civil Rights Act in 1964, making it illegal to treat people differently based on the color of their skin, on their religious beliefs or whether they are a man or woman.

The law means that schools, work places, restaurants and hotels must treat all people the same. The team started changing too. Five years after the Pirates won the World Series, the team had nine blacks and Latinos on a roster of twenty-five men.

More than ever, Roberto wanted to be the best. He still wanted to prove that someone with dark skin and a Spanish accent could be the most valuable player in the major leagues. He had heard stories about Babe Ruth, the Yankees' famous slugger from the 1920s and 1930s.

Roberto earned the Golden Glove Award many times
for being the best right fielder of the season

"Always, they said Babe Ruth was the best
there was," Roberto said. "They said you'd really have to be something to be like Babe Ruth.
But Babe Ruth was an American player. What
we needed was a Puerto Rican player they could
say that about, someone to look up to and try
to equal."

After the 1960 World Series, Roberto played
so well the next season that the other players
voted for him to start the All-Star game in right
field. He finished the season with the Silver Bat
award for having the best batting average in the

National League and the Golden Glove for being among the three best outfielders.

Roberto had the league's best batting average again in 1964 and 1965. And he started winning the Golden Glove every year. People were noticing his ability.

During the offseason, Roberto kept playing for his Puerto Rican team too. One year when the team played in the Inter-American World Series in the country of Nicaragua, a fan dropped a large lizard over the fence in right field. Roberto ran away screaming. He was afraid of lizards.

A fan dropped a lizard onto the field, terrifying Roberto, who ran away screaming

But it was not always easy for Roberto to keep playing baseball and to always play at a high level. His back and neck still hurt. Sometimes he got sick too. Before the 1965 season, Roberto caught a tropical disease called malaria. He ended up back in the hospital and lost twenty-five pounds before the season.

Roberto realized he had to eat good foods to stay healthy. He ate lots of vegetables and fruit smoothies. He made a habit of never eating too much either. He would stop eating before getting too full.

Early in his career, Roberto did not hit a lot of home runs. Instead, he studied how the ball bounced in different stadiums. He would hit the ball into play and then run hard. He knew that the longer the ball rolled across the grass, he would have more time to keep running among the base paths.

One time, Roberto set a league record by getting ten hits in a row, over two games. He also figured out how to stretch the bases, turning a single into a double or a double into a triple. He would run fast, testing players in the field and challenging them to get him out. Once he had three triples in a game.

Always, he continued to communicate with his body. Even when he was not swinging a bat or chasing the ball, he thought about how he looked to the fans. Roberto walked with his back straight and his head high. He knew that sent the message that he appreciated the fans and wanted to do his best. By 1966, most Pirates players from the World Series team were gone. The team manager met with Roberto before the season. He wanted Roberto to hit the ball harder. So he did.

In the field, Roberto kept getting better too. Fans said that Roberto's fingertips seemed to have eyes because of the way he could grab the ball off a tough bounce. And his arm continued to impress. "Clemente could field the ball in New York and throw out a guy in Pennsylvania," one announcer joked.

Roberto stopped being so quiet and shy too. He always had pushed himself to play hard.

Now he started pushing other players too—for themselves, for their teammates and for the city of Pittsburgh and its fans. He wanted the entire team to reach its potential and play its best.

The Pirates finished the 1966 season with ninety-two wins and seventy losses. The team had played great, but it still finished three games behind the Dodgers, who won the pennant and represented the National League in the World Series.

Roberto had his best season ever. He set personal records for home runs, runs batted in and runs scored. He had hit harder and his batting average had dropped only a little.

People close to Roberto believe he had been the league's most valuable player. "No man ever gave more of himself or worked more unselfishly for the good of the team than Roberto," his manager said after the season.

Only the sports reporters would determine who was most valuable though. When the votes were counted, Roberto received 218 votes—or ten more than the next best guy.

BOB CLEMENTE outfield

Roberto is remembered on baseball cards as
Bob Clemente, Pirates outfielder and MVP

For the first time in his career, Roberto was the league's most valuable player. It was also the first time a Latino player was the most valuable. Roberto had set his goal high, he had worked hard and he had achieved success. After that, people started calling Roberto "The Great One."

When he won the award, Roberto believed it might inspire other boys from Puerto Rico and Latin America to dream of playing baseball in the United States. "This makes me happy because now I feel that if I could do it, then they could do it," Roberto said. "The kids have someone to look up to and to follow. I show them what baseball has done for me, and maybe they will work harder and try harder and be better men."

Chapter 7
Leaving It All

Roberto stayed humble after being named most valuable. He kept visiting friends in the old neighborhood. When people stopped him on the island, he stayed to talk. He made time for the fans.

Roberto believed he had to be a good father to his three sons too. One year on Father's Day, he wrote a poem that ended with the line: "What else can I ask if I know that my sons really love me?"

He could ask himself to keep getting better. And he did. The most important thing Roberto did as a father was spend time with his boys. When they traveled to Puerto Rico in the winters, Roberto took his sons with him everywhere he went.

Even after Roberto became a star, he still took time to teach the basics of the game to young boys in Pittsburgh and back in Puerto Rico. His own boys watched how their father carried himself with his head high. He treated even strangers with respect and friendliness.

Roberto enjoyed teaching children
about baseball and often offered free lessons
if he saw kids playing on one of his visits

When the family was in Pittsburgh, Roberto often took his sons to the ballpark. One year on family day, he dressed all three boys in matching Pirates uniforms with his number 21 and took them on the field before the game. It was as if he was introducing his sons to the fans in Pittsburgh. The fans loved it, cheering for Roberto and for his family. They had fully embraced Roberto as a baseball player and as a person.

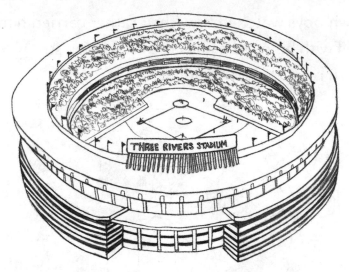

The Three Rivers Stadium opened in 1970
and sported turf, which was unfamiliar to Roberto,
instead of grass

In 1970, the Pirates moved into a modern, con-
crete stadium. Instead of grass, it had artificial
turf, stretching like a green carpet over the field.
The Pirates had changed too. Roberto had been
one of four players on the 1960 team who were
not white. But now, blacks and Latinos made up
a majority of the team.

By the next year, 1971, Roberto's team was
back in the World Series. On September 1 of that
year, the Pirates became the first Major League
Baseball team to field a starting lineup without a

single white player. It had been twenty-four years since Jackie Robinson became the first African American in the league.

That year, the Baltimore Orioles won the American League championship. Again, almost everyone expected the Pirates to lose. Baltimore had won the World Series the year before and

The Baltimore Orioles were the favorite for the 1971 World Series, but they would have to go through the Pirates, and Roberto, to get it

it had strong pitchers. Pittsburgh would be the underdog again.

After the Orioles easily won the first two games of the series, it seemed the predictions were accurate. Roberto was not ready to quit. At thirty-seven years old, he was the oldest player on either team. In the Pirates' locker room after the second game, he spoke up. When he first came into the league, he had been shy and uncertain about speaking English. Now he was a leader. "Hold on," he told the team, "we're gonna do it."

Even at his age, Roberto ran hard on every play. Some baseball experts said his running changed the series. In Game 3 at Pittsburgh's new Three Rivers Stadium, Roberto hit a dribbler back to the pitcher. But he ran fast. That made the pitcher hurry and he missed the throw to first. Roberto was safe. That play started a Pirates rally. They won that game and the next two games to lead the series.

In Pittsburgh, the Pirates had hosted the first-ever night game for the World Series. Until that point, every other game had been played during the day. More than 50,000 people attended the game, and more than sixty-one million watched at home—the largest-ever TV audience at that time.

As they headed back to Baltimore, the Pirates needed just one more win. When the Orioles took the next game, the World Series once more came down to the seventh game. Winner takes all. Loser goes home. "Don't worry," Roberto told his teammates before the game. "We are gonna win this game. No problem."

He didn't just talk either. Roberto hit a solo home run with two outs in the fourth inning. He had gotten a hit in all fourteen World Series games in which he played. The Pirates scored another run late in the game, and Baltimore scored just one run in the bottom half of the eighth inning. The Pirates were World Series champions again.

Roberto had a .414 batting average over the series and he had played strong defense. This time, when the sports writers chose a World Series MVP, they picked him. He won a new car, a Dodge Charger.

With his World Series MVP trophy, Roberto also won a new 1971 Dodge Charger

As the reporters gathered around Roberto to ask him how it felt to be the most valuable player, he asked their permission to say something in Spanish first. He still remembered the people back home, on his island. "On the greatest day of my life," he said in Spanish, "I bless my children and I ask my parents for their blessing."

Switching back to English, Roberto told the reporters that for the first time in his career, he had no regrets about the way he played. He had left everything on the field. He had played as well as he could. And he had walked off the field as a champion.

When Roberto came into the league twenty years earlier, people made fun of his Spanish accent. They treated him badly because of his dark skin. He seemed different. Over the years, he changed people's impressions and attitudes.

Everyone wanted to interview Roberto after his MVP win. No one was making fun of him for his accent now

Roberto had played hard. He had held his head high, even when people made fun of him. He had stayed true to himself and what he believed. And the people had seen him for what he was, a great ballplayer and a leader off the field too.

Roberto still had his big dream. He wanted to build his sports city. In his mind, it would have three baseball fields, a swimming pool, basketball courts and tennis courts, and a lake where parents and children could go together.

Roberto knew he could not build it alone. The project would take lots of money and he would need help. But he would spend every day working toward his goal.

"If you have a chance to accomplish something that will make things better for people coming behind you, and you don't do that," he often said, "you are wasting your time on this earth."

Chapter 8
<u>Getting on Board</u>

Fans started asking Roberto when he planned to retire from baseball, but he wasn't ready to be done. He still had a couple of goals to reach. He wanted to reach 3,000 hits. Only ten players had gotten that many hits before. Roberto figured if he stayed healthy and had a good season, he had a chance to get there too.

Late in the 1972 season, Roberto stroked a double off of the left field wall. It was the 3,000th hit of his career. He stood on second base and tipped his hat in gratitude. As he looked around the gigantic baseball stadium, Roberto could see all kinds of people—whites, African Americans, Latinos, Spanish-speakers and English-speakers, young and old—standing and cheering for him.

The world had changed. Roberto had helped people see that what mattered most was how he played the game and how he treated people when he wasn't playing. They were cheering for him because of everything he had done.

"What it means is I didn't fail with the ability I had," Roberto said after the game. "I've seen lots of players come and leave. Some failed because they didn't have the ability. And some failed because they didn't have the desire."

Roberto tipped his hat to his fans after his 3,000th hit, the eleventh player in history to reach that milestone

The Pirates had only three games left in the season and the manager planned to rest Roberto for the playoffs. But someone with the team realized that Roberto had a chance to hit one more milestone. If he played in just one more game, Roberto could tie the record for most games played by a Pirate.

He appeared one more time that season. That meant he had played in 2,433 games. It seemed hard to believe that teammates had long ago ac-

After he played his last game, he tipped his hat again as he broke the record for most Pirates games played

cused Roberto of "jaking it"—or faking injuries so he wouldn't have to play.

The Pirates finished with ninety-six wins and the best record in the National League. By then, Major League Baseball had adopted a playoff system. The Pirates played the Cincinnati Reds in the National League Championship Series and lost. They would not return to the World Series.

Roberto went back home to Puerto Rico. He was asked to coach the island's team in the Amateur Baseball World Series in Nicaragua. He remembered being there years before when a fan dropped a lizard over the right field fence.

Roberto liked Nicaragua because it reminded him of Puerto Rico when he was a child. The people did not have as much money or new buildings and many paved roads. Many were poor, working in the country and living simple lives. When Roberto saw them, he remembered what it had been like living in his parents' little wooden house, with his brothers, sisters and cousins sleeping in every room.

Roberto remembered his mother working hard to butcher meat and to cook over the outside stove, making food to sell to the workers. He remembered his father leaving the house many mornings before sunrise to stay all day in the sugarcane fields. Roberto felt like he understood these poor people in Nicaragua. And the people there looked up to him. He quickly fell in love with the country.

Puerto Rico won nine games in the tournament, including a no-hitter, but finished tied for sixth place. Roberto headed back home to his island to celebrate Christmas with his wife, sons, parents and extended family. Two days before the holiday, Roberto heard the news and became worried. An earthquake had hit the capital of Nicaragua. Seven thousand people died, and a quarter-million more lost their homes.

Roberto thought about all of the friends he had made in Nicaragua. Some of the people he had met would be dead. Others would be homeless. Many more would need food and medicine. Roberto asked what the people needed. The answer came back that they needed everything. He agreed to help.

He formed a committee to raise money, and he even went door-to-door in Puerto Rico asking people to donate. He raised $150,000. It was enough money to purchase twenty-six tons of food, clothing and medicine. The committee rented an airplane and started flying the supplies to Nicaragua.

But Roberto started hearing that the items were not getting to the people who needed them. Nicaragua's military dictator sent his troops to wait for the airplanes. They were taking the best items for themselves and leaving poor people to starve and die.

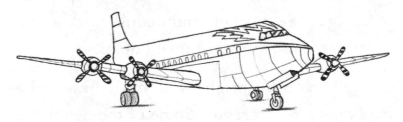

The DC-7 that was supposed to take Roberto
to Nicaragua had tiger stripes and lightning bolts
painted on it and, though he was scared,
Roberto got in

That made Roberto angry. He vowed to travel there himself and make sure the supplies got to the people. Even though it was New Year's Eve and people on the island would be celebrating with fireworks and parties, Roberto did not want to wait.

He talked with the pilot of another plane about making a trip to Nicaragua. The pilot agreed to take him and a load of supplies. The plane looked nice. The pilot had painted it a silvery white and added orange-and-black lightning bolts near the cockpit and tiger stripes on the propellers.

But Roberto did not know the old plane, called a DC-7, had problems. Not all of the sparkplugs in the engines would fire. The propellers had been damaged in an accident. The pilot who agreed to take him was not qualified to fly the plane.

Even when the crew started loading the supplies, they did not know how to do it. They packed in bags of rice, cans of evaporated milk and cartons of beans. But they put on too much stuff. The plane was overloaded and the cargo was unbalanced.

A friend stood on the tarmac with Roberto and looked at the plane. The tires looked like they were squished from all the weight, and the plane seemed to be tilting back. He warned Roberto not to get on board.

Roberto had been afraid of flying for years. He often dreamed he would die in a plane crash. When the Pirates took long flights, he sometimes shouted out a prayer when the plane hit bumpy turbulence. But he also knew the people in Nicaragua desperately needed his help. He turned to his wife and told her not to worry.

Many people helped search for the missing plane, but only some debris was found

"When your time comes, it comes," he told her. "If you are going to die, you will die. And babies are dying. They need these supplies." He kissed her goodbye and climbed onto the plane.

The DC-7 moved slowly down the runway and it took off into the air but barely passed over the palm trees near the airport. The plane banked out over the ocean and quickly started coming back down. The engines had stopped working. The plane hit the water as if it had run into a brick wall. It broke apart and disappeared beneath the water.

When the first news reports came across the radio saying a plane had crashed, Vera did not believe it could be Roberto's plane. But then she knew it had to be.

Roberto's friends and admirers had trouble believing he was gone too. Most people found out about the crash on New Year's Eve, amid the parties and celebrations. By morning, thousands of people stood along the shoreline in Puerto Rico, looking out at the water where the plane had disappeared. Some started walking into the waves, as if they could just reach out and pull him back.

U.S. Navy deep sea divers spent days looking for the plane. Manny Sanguillen, Roberto's teammate and friend, joined them, going below the surface over and over. Eventually, the crews located parts of the plane and its engines. No one ever found Roberto's body.

A message lit up the hill overlooking Pittsburgh as fans mourned the loss of Roberto

People in Puerto Rico, in Pittsburgh, throughout the United States and across Latin America mourned the loss of a hero. Roberto led by example while he was alive, and he died while trying to help others.

The governor of Puerto Rico came to the house to see Vera and the boys. Teammates came from Pittsburgh. Fans came from Venezuela, the Dominican Republic and the United States. They all wanted to tell Vera and Roberto's sons how much he had meant to their lives.

A large sign on the hill overlooking Pittsburgh lit up at night, saying: "Adios, Amigo Roberto."

Roberto Jr, Vera, Luis Clemente and family friend Modesto Lacen were invited to PNC Park to celebrate the 40th anniversary of Roberto's 3,000th hit

Goodbye, friend. A Pittsburgh newspaper compared Roberto to a knight in shining armor. The paper recalled how he had not given in to the people who saw only his skin color or heard only his Spanish accent. He had set a positive example and helped others.

"The poor people whom he helped during his lifetime—the children, the elderly, the downtrodden, the unfortunate whom he often gave a helping hand to get a new lease on life—may not have a Hall of Fame for all to see," the paper wrote. "But to them, Roberto Clemente will never be forgotten, for they have an indelible imprint of Roberto Clemente in their hearts."

Roberto's parents both lived longer than their son. When he died, his half-brother, Luis, already had died from cancer and his half-sister, Rosa, had died while giving birth. His oldest brother Osvaldo had died in 1960 and his sister, Anairis, had died at age five. Roberto's other brothers lived many years: Justino died at age eighty-five and Andres died at seventy-two.

Roberto Clemente Jr. kisses a painting of his dad
at a memorial after the plane crash

Vera Clemente continues to carry on her husband's legacy by volunteering her time to help others and attending ceremonies in Roberto's memory. Roberto's sons missed their father after he died and had a hard time understanding where he had gone. They have carried forward his message of helping others. They work hard to make their father's dreams reality too.

Roberto Jr. lives near Houston, but visits Pittsburgh and Puerto Rico often. He works on brain research to protect athletes from concussions and help detect illnesses in adults. The other sons—Luis and Enrique—work at Sports City, an athletic complex on the island, helping introduce new generations of Puerto Ricans to athletics. They are planning to expand and update the sports complex.

Chapter 9
<u>Living On</u>

As soon as Roberto died, the members of the Baseball Writers' Association of America started talking about waiving the rule that a player had to be inactive for five years before entering the National Baseball Hall of Fame.

Over his career, Roberto had won twelve Gold Glove awards as a top National League outfielder. He won four batting titles, as the best hitter in

Roberto will always be remembered as
a great hitter and a tremendous right fielder
who set many records for latino players

the league. His lifetime batting average was .317. He had won two World Series championships.

He was the 1966 Most Valuable Player. And he had been the World Series MVP in 1971. The writers knew, without waiting, that Roberto deserved to be in the hall of fame.

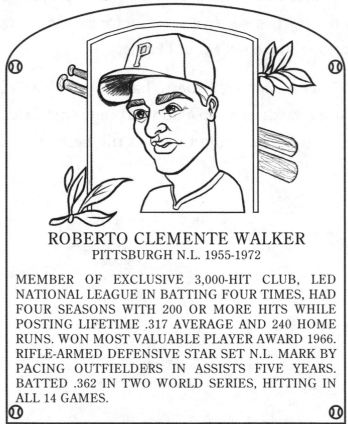

ROBERTO CLEMENTE WALKER
PITTSBURGH N.L. 1955-1972

MEMBER OF EXCLUSIVE 3,000-HIT CLUB, LED NATIONAL LEAGUE IN BATTING FOUR TIMES, HAD FOUR SEASONS WITH 200 OR MORE HITS WHILE POSTING LIFETIME .317 AVERAGE AND 240 HOME RUNS. WON MOST VALUABLE PLAYER AWARD 1966. RIFLE-ARMED DEFENSIVE STAR SET N.L. MARK BY PACING OUTFIELDERS IN ASSISTS FIVE YEARS. BATTED .362 IN TWO WORLD SERIES, HITTING IN ALL 14 GAMES.

His National Baseball Hall of Fame plaque
details Roberto's accomplishments
throughout his baseball career

Pittsburgh's mayor ordered the observance of Roberto Clemente Week in the city, and officials hung a picture of Roberto in the lobby of city hall. "The tragic death of Roberto Clemente has saddened Pittsburgh and the entire nation," the mayor wrote to Vera and the boys.

U.S. President Richard Nixon praised Roberto and gave one thousand dollars of his own money to the Nicaraguan relief effort. Puerto Rico's governor spoke for the people of the island: "The hearts of all of us are in sorrow."

In one of this last interviews before he died, Roberto talked about the frustrations he had felt during his life. It had been hard coming to the United States and being treated differently because he had dark skin and because he could not speak English clearly.

He wanted people to know that as important as baseball had been to him, he felt even more strongly about being a role model off the field. He wanted people to understand his whole story. "I'm a man first and a baseball player next," Roberto had said. "Treat me that way."

When people wanted to send flowers for a church service to mark Roberto's death, Vera suggested they send donations instead. Her husband had dreamed of building a sports city for the children of Puerto Rico. It had become her dream too.

She created the Roberto Clemente Foundation for Youth. People sent letters, sometimes with just a few dollars. Other times, they sent large donations. A bank and newspaper in Puerto Rico started the fund with a $25,000 donation.

The Roberto Clemente Sports City opened within two years. It covers more than three hundred acres with fields for baseball, football and soccer, a swimming pool, tennis courts and

Roberto's dream of building a sports city finally came true and it is now run by his two youngest sons

basketball courts. More than 200,000 children per year go there to play, learn and train.

Sports City has produced Major League Baseball players such as brothers Roberto and Sandy Alomar, Juan Gonzalez, Ivan Rodriguez and Ruben Sierra, among others. Decades after he died, Roberto's legacy continues in the people who followed his example, the ones who still tell his story and those who read about it.

Roberto and Sandy Alomar benefitted from
Clemente's Sports City and made it into
Major League baseball themselves

His name appears on schools and hospitals, on the main stadium in San Juan, Puerto Rico, and on a Pittsburgh bridge next to the Pirates' stadium, PNC Park. A larger-than-life statue of Roberto, showing him running toward first base after hitting a ball, stands outside the Pittsburgh ballpark.

The Roberto Clemente Bridge in Pittsburgh is right next to the current Pirates stadium and reminds people everyday of his fight for equality

Major League Baseball gives out a Roberto Clemente Award each year to a player who supports his community and helps others. "He not only was a great baseball player but most importantly he was actually a person who cared for others," his son Roberto Jr. said. "He left a great fingerprint. Not only in the game of baseball but in society."

The statue of Roberto Clemente was originally outside Three Rivers Stadium but was moved to PNC Park where it stands with other Hall-of-Fame players

Select Quotes from Roberto Clemente

"I want to be remembered as a ballplayer who gave all he had to give."
    – Clemente comment.

"I don't believe in color, I believe in people. I always respect everyone, and thanks to God, my mother and my father taught me never to hate, never to dislike someone because of their color."
    – Clemente commenting on color in an interview.

"I believe that every human being is equal, but one has to fight hard all the time to maintain that equality."
    – Clemente in one of his speeches.

"Always, they said Babe Ruth was the best there was. They said you'd really have to be something to be like Babe Ruth. But Babe Ruth was an American player. What we needed was a Puerto Rican player they could say that about, someone to look up to and try to equal."
    – Clemente's comment about trying to be the best player ever.

"If you have a chance to accomplish something that will make things better for people coming behind you, and you don't do that, you are wasting your time on this earth."
    – Clemente was committed to positive change.

"I'm a man first and a baseball player next. Treat me that way."
    – Clemente in one of his last interviews wanted people to see him as a role model.

Roberto Clemente Timeline

1934 August 18   Born in Barrio San Antón, Carolina, Puerto Rico

1952 October 9   Becomes a professional baseball player, by signing a contract to play with a winter league team in Puerto Rico

1952 November 6   Tries out for the Brooklyn Dodgers in Puerto Rico

1954 February 19   Signs a contract to play minor league baseball for the Brooklyn Dodgers

1954 November 22   Pittsburgh Pirates pick Clemente with the team's first selection of the rookie draft

1955 April 17   Plays in his first Major League Baseball game, with the Pirates

1960 October 13   Becomes first Latino to win a World Series as a starter

1964 November 14   Marries Vera Zabala

1965 August 17   His son Roberto Jr. is born

1966 July 13   A second son, Luis Roberto, is born

1966   Becomes first Latino to win the National League Most Valuable Player award

1970   A third son, Enrique Roberto, is born

1971 October 17   Becomes first Latino to be named the World Series Most Valuable Player when the Pirates defeat the heavily favored Baltimore Orioles

1972 September 30   Becomes the 11th player in Major League Baseball history to have 3,000 hits

1972 December 31   Dies on New Year's Eve in a plane crash off the coast of San Juan, Puerto Rico, while on a trip to deliver aid to earthquake victims in Nicaragua

World Timeline

1934   Babe Ruth signs $35,000 contract with New York Yankees

1942 April 21   Hiram Bithorn becomes the first Puerto Rican to play in Major League Baseball

1947 January 3   The Crawford-Butler act allows Puerto Rican citizens to elect their own governor instead of having one appointed to them

1947 April 15   Jackie Robinson becomes the first African American to play in Major League Baseball

1950 June 25   Korean War starts, remaining an active conflict until 1953

1951   Joe DiMaggio announces his retirement

1952   First black umpire in organized baseball, Emmett Ashford, is certified

1954 May 17   The U.S. Supreme Court rules in the case Brown v. Board of Education that separate schools for black and white students are unconstitutional

1959   The Vietnam War starts

1960 October 13   Bill Mazeroski wins the World Series for the Pirates with a game seven walk off

1963 August 28   The March on Washington protest for civil rights calls for change

1965 December 9   Branch Rickey, the Pirates manager, dies

1968 April 4   Civil Rights leader Martin Luther King, Jr. is assassinated in Memphis, Tennessee

1972 April 1   The United States baseball strike begins

1972 October 24   Jackie Robinson dies

Roberto Clemente Timeline (cont.)

1973 August 6   Inducted into the National Baseball Hall of Fame, after members of the Baseball Writers Association of America grant an exception to the rule that a player must be inactive five years to be eligible. He is the first Latino in the Hall

<u>World Timeline</u> (cont.)

1972 December 23   An earthquake hits the Nicaraguan capital of Managua. Seven thousand people are killed. More than 250,000 lose their homes

1975 April 30   Vietnam War ends

Glossary

Affiliate   A related group; in baseball, the minor league team a major league team sponsors

Batting average   A baseball statistic, it is a percentage based on the number of hits a batter gets divided by the number of times he goes to bat

Breadfruit   A type of fruit that grows on trees in the Caribbean with a spiky green exterior and a white starchy inside that looks and tastes similar to potato when cooked

Caribbean   A region of about 700 islands scattered over 1 million square miles southeast of the mainland United States. It includes 13 countries and 17 territories that are aligned with other countries

Cologne   A perfume typically worn by men

Dictator   Ruler with total power, who often leads by force

Diploma   A piece of paper awarded to someone when they graduate from a school

Dormitory   A place where people live together, often while in school

Foreman   A head worker or boss who oversees other workers

Golden Glove   An award given at the end of the season to the best fielder at each position in the American and National leagues

Great Depression   The economic crisis and period of low business activity in the United States and other countries beginning with the stock-market crash in 1929 and continuing through most of the 1930s.

Major League Baseball   The highest level of professional baseball in North America now, with 29 teams in the United States and the Toronto Blue Jays in Canada, divided into the American and National leagues

Microcosm   A small thing that illustrates or exemplifies something larger

Mofongo   A Puerto Rican dish made with plantains, vegetables and sometimes a meat such as crab, shrimp or chicken

Morcilla   A Puerto Rican sausage made with blood, spices and sometimes rice

MVP   The Most Valuable Player award given to one player in each of the American and National leagues, chosen by the Baseball Writers Association of America

National Baseball Hall of Fame   A museum in Cooperstown, New York, that tells the history of baseball and enshrines the best players from Major League Baseball

Negro Leagues   Baseball leagues for African American players that existed before the Major Leagues started including African Americans

Plantains   A starchy fruit similar to a banana

Puerto Rico   A Caribbean territory of the United States with about 3.7 million people acquired from Spain in 1898 after the Spanish-American War

Racism   discrimination, different treatment, or hatred based on race or skin color

RBI   Runs batted in; a baseball statistic counting how many points a batter generates off of his hits

Silver Bat   An award given to one hitter with the highest batting average in the American and National leagues

Silver Slugger   An award given to the hitter with the highest batting average at each position in the American and National leagues. Major League Baseball started giving out this award in 1980, after Roberto Clemente died

Tarmac   The pavement on an airport runway

Yuca   Also known as cassava, the root can be boiled or fried with a look and taste similar to potato

Bibliography

Clemente Family, The. *Clemente: The True Legacy of an Undying Hero.* New York: Celebra, 2013.

Major League Baseball. www.MLB.com.

Maranis, David. *Clemente: The Passion and Grace of Baseball's Last Hero.* New York: Simon & Schuster, 2006.

National Baseball Hall of Fame. www.basballhall.org.

Senator John Heinz History Center and Western Pennsylvania Sports Museum. www.heinzhistorycenter.org.

Smithsonian Institution Traveling Exhibition Service. "Beyond Baseball: The Life of Roberto Clemente." www.robertoclemente.si.edu.

Wagenheim, Kal. *Clemente!* Santa Barbara, CA: Praeger Publishers, 1973.

Walker, Paul Robert. *Pride of Puerto Rico: The Life of Roberto Clemente.* Boston: Houghton Mifflin Harcourt, 1991.

Further Reading

Darraj, Susan Muaddi. *Roberto Clemente: The Great Hispanic Heritage.* New York: Chelsea Hosue Publications, 2008.

Engle, Trudie. *We'll Never Forget You, Roberto Clemente.* New York: Scholastic, 1997.

Gigliotti, Jim. *I Am: Roberto Clemente.* Boston: Houghton Mifflin Harcourt, 1991.

Special thanks to Roberto Clemente Jr.

Index

A
accent, difficulty of, 45. See also English
activist, 62
All-Star game, 65
Alomar, Roberto, 99
Alomar, Sandy, 99
Amateur Baseball World Series, 84
American League, 48-49, 75
awards
    Golden Glove, 65, 66, 108
    Silver Bat, 65, 110

B
back injuries, 43, 44, 67
Baltimore Orioles, 75–77
baseball
    equipment as a child, 6, 7, 8
    frustration with, 18
    hard work put into, 13
    locker, 29, 38
    love of the game, 8
    making money from, ix
    teaching, 72, 73
    turning pro, 14–23
Baseball Writers' Association of America, 95
batting average
    1971 World Series, 77
    improvement in, 43
Bernier, Carlos, 20
Big Crab, 14
birthplace (of Roberto Clemente), 1
black players, treatment of, 62, 63
Brooklyn Dodgers, 15-20, 69

C
Cangrejeros de Santurce (Santurce Crabbers), 14-20, 24
car accident, injuries from, 43
career hits, 81
Cathedral of Learning skyscraper, 29

Civil Rights, 62, 63
Civil Rights Act in 1964, 64
Clemente family
    Clemente, Anairis (sister), 5, 92
    Clemente, Andres (brother), 4, 92
    Clemente, Justino (brother), 4, 92
    Clemente, Melchor (father), 2-4, 11, 12, 16
    Clemente, Osvaldo (brother), 4, 92
    Clemente, Vera Cristina Zabala (wife), 58–61, 85, 88, 89, 91,
    Oquendo, Luis (half-brother), 3, 92
    Walker, Luisa (mother), 3, 4
crash, airplane, 88-90

D
DC-7 airplane, 86, 87, 88, 89
discrimination, 26–28, 34, 61
drafts, 1-19, 22
dreams, teaching people to follow, 36

E
earthquakes, 85
English, speaking, 17, 28, 31-33, 36, 43, 76, 97
equality, 36, 37, 62, 63, 100, 103

F
factories, 25, 26
family, 2-6, 59, 60, 61, 73
fan letters, 39, 40
fear of flying, 88
Florida
    Civil Rights in, 26, 63
    practice in, 25
    spring training, 62
food from home, 32
Forbes, John, 28, 29
Forbes Field, 29, 30, 48, 50

G
Golden Glove award, 65, 66, 103
Gonzalez, Juan, 99
Great Depression, 5, 6, 108
The Great One, 71

I
Inter-American World Series, 66
Irvin, Monte, 8, 10

J

jíbaro, 35

K

King, Martin Luther, 62, 63
Korean War, 57, 105

L

Latino athletes
    encouragement of, 37, 39
    first player to win MVP, 70, 77
locker, 29, 38
Louisville Slugger bats, 16

M

Major League Baseball (MLB), 5, 15, 19, 20, 29, 37, 42, 48, 60,
    64, 74, 84, 99, 100, 109
marriage, 59
Mays, Willie, 18
Mazeroski, Bill, 52-55
military training, 57, 58
Milwaukee Braves, 15
money, 35–41
Montreal Royals, 16-18
Most Valuable Player (MVP), 57–71, 77, 78, 79, 96, 109

N

National Baseball Hall of Fame, 39, 92, 95, 96, 101, 106, 109
National League, 48, 49, 66, 69, 84, 95
neck injuries, 43, 67
New York Yankees
    1960 World Series, 49–55
    Ruth, Babe, 64
Nicaragua, 66, 84
    earthquake in, 85
    flight to, 87

P

pain, playing in, 43-45, 67
pennant races, 47-49, 69
performance, 42–56
Pittsburgh, Pennsylvania, 24, 25, 52, 60, 72, 73, 90, 91
    Forbes Field, 29, 30
    Roberto Clemente Bridge, 100
Pittsburgh Pirates, 19, 20
    1960 season, 47–50

1966 season, 68, 69
    becoming a Pirate, 24–34
    draft of Robert, 22, 23
    most games played as, 83
    scouts, 21
PNC Park, statue at, 101
Prince, Bill, 45, 46
Puerto Rico, vii, 1, 35
    after plane crash, 89-91
    after winning 1960 World Series, 56
    food from home, 32
    life in, 1-11
    map of, viii, 1
    return to, x, 18, 35-37, 84
    Roberto Clemente Sports City, 41, 94, 98-99
    winters in, 18, 72

R

Rickey, Branch, 20, 22
Roberto Clemente Bridge, 100
Roberto Clemente Foundation, 98
Roberto Clemente Sports City, 98-99
Roberts, Curt, 20
Robinson, Jackie, 20, 21, 37, 75
Rodriguez, Ivan, 99
Ruth, Babe, 64, 65

S

San Juan Senadores (Senators), 8
Santurce Crabbers (Cangrejeros de Santurce), 14, 15, 18, 19, 24
scouts, 17, 18
    Brooklyn Dodgers, 15
    Pittsburgh Pirates, 20
segregation, 26-28
Sello Rojo softball team, 11
shirt number (21), 31, 73
Sierra, Ruben, 99
Silver Bat award, 65, 110
Spanish, speaking, vii, 17, 20, 28, 39, 56, 78

T

territories, United States, 1
Three Rivers Stadium, 74, 76
three thousandth hit, 81, 82
toughness, questioned by teammates, 44

U

United States territories, 1
University of Pittsburgh, 30
U.S. Marines, 57, 58

W

World Series, 48, 69, 84
    1960, 49–56, 64, 65
    1971, 74-77
    Amateur Baseball World Series, 84-85
    first night game of, 76
    Inter-American, 66
    Most Valuable Player (MVP), 19, 77-80, 96

Y

YMCA, encouragement to young athletes, 40